Untangling the Web

A Beginner's Guide to Political Science on the World Wide Web

UNTANGLING THE WEB

A Beginner's Guide to Political Science on the World Wide Web

Brian Werner
ST. JOHN'S UNIVERSITY, NEW YORK

St. Martin's Press
New York

Sponsoring editors: Beth Gillett, Ted Whitten
Development editors: Ted Whitten, Meg Spilleth
Managing editor: Patricia Mansfield Phelan
Senior project editor: Erica Appel
Art director: Lucy Krikorian
Text and cover design: Patricia McFadden

Manufactured in the United States of America.

1 0 9 8 7
f e d c b

For information, write:
St. Martin's Press, Inc.
175 Fifth Avenue
New York, NY 10010

ISBN: 0-312-15257-4

CONTENTS

PREFACE

Untangling the Web is intended to help students and instructors use the numerous sources of information on government and politics available on the World Wide Web (WWW). It was written in conjunction with the St. Martin's Press College Division Web Site to teach students the basics of exploring the Web and its vast store of information concerning American government and politics.

The first part, Welcome to the World Wide Web, guides students (and instructors!) through the basics of navigating the Web using a Web browser. The second part, Researching Politics on the Web, offers advice and strategies for conducting Web research efficiently and effectively. The section entitled St. Martin's Political Science Supplements on the World Wide Web introduces students to the Web supplements for three American Government textbooks published by St. Martin's Press: *The Politics of American Government* by Stephen Wayne, G. Calvin Mackenzie, David M. O'Brien, and Richard L. Cole; *A Delicate Balance* by Paul Light; and *The Play of Power* by James Eisenstein, Mark Kessler, Bruce A. Williams, and Jacqueline Vaughn Switzer. Through these texts, their supplements, and our extensive Web site, St. Martin's brings the world of politics into the classroom. Check out the St. Martin's Web site at:

http://www.smpcollege.com/smp_govt/

INSTRUCTORS

What do instructors need to do to use the Web supplement?

You don't have to be a Web expert to use St. Martin's Political Science Supplements on the World Wide Web. If you are teaching American Government using a St. Martin's Press textbook, you can use the supplemental Web materials that link the lessons of the textbook to brief research exercises on the World Wide Web. To get your students started on the Web, contact your computer center and tell them that your students need: (1) information about where on campus they can use computers that connect them to the World Wide Web using a graphical browser such as Netscape Navigator, (2) brief instructions on connecting to the World Wide Web, and (3) mainframe computer accounts and e-mail addresses (if you want assignments e-mailed to you).

This guidebook will get even the least computer literate students online and doing political science research on the Web in a matter of minutes. The exercises promote writing and research skills, computer literacy, and empirical knowledge of political science.

You can choose from over 100 Web research exercises to assign to your students. The students will use the St. Martin's Political Science Links Page (a list of political science reference sources) to find Web resources around the world. They will gather information and be prompted to write brief reports that can be printed out or sent directly to your e-mail address.

STUDENTS

What do students need to do to use the Web supplement?

Even if you've never used the Web before, you can quickly learn how to find an incredible amount of information on government and politics. This guide will take you step-by-step onto the Web, give you the basics of getting around, and teach you how to find what you want efficiently.

If you're not using your own computer, your instructor can tell you where to go on campus to find computers that can connect to the Web. Either your instructor or the computing center can give you quick instructions on how to connect to the Web. Your instructor will provide you with the Web address of St. Martin's Press and perhaps his or her e-mail address.

Unless you're using your own computer with a hard disk drive, you will need a blank 3.5-inch floppy disk with 1.4 megabytes of storage space. You can buy this at your campus bookstore or at any computer supply store. You will use this disk to copy information from the Web, store your written assignments, and keep track of interesting places on the Web that you may want to visit again.

Your instructor will assign Web research exercises. You will use the St. Martin's Political Science Links Page to search Web resources around the world. You will be asked to write and submit brief reports either in print or by e-mail to your instructor.

WELCOME TO THE WORLD WIDE WEB

Welcome to the study of politics on the World Wide Web! This guide will take you from your textbook to the vast political resources of the Web. If you are a **newbie*** to the Web, this guide will quickly have you crawling the Web with confidence, ready to discover its wealth of information on government and politics. Experienced **surfers** can use this guide for a quick orientation to political research on the Web and for details on the supplemental Web research assignments by skipping ahead to the section entitled "Researching Politics on the Web."

There are many ways to connect with the Web. You may be using your school's computer or your own. You may be using a software program, called a **browser**, from Netscape, Mosaic, America Online, or one of the dozens of other options. The instructions and examples in this guide are based on the most popular browser, Netscape's Navigator 2.01, and may not predict exactly how the Web will appear to you. Almost all of the features described can be found with other browsers as well. Whatever browser you use, you'll find what you need; but what you see on your screen might look slightly different from what the other students see on theirs.

WHAT IS THE WEB?

The World Wide Web is a vast array of information stored in the files of computers at colleges and universities, government offices, businesses, nonprofit organizations, computer services, and the homes of people around the world. These computer files all use the same computer language (HTML) and are connected by phone lines. When your computer contacts one of these computers using a **modem**, the other computer (the **server**) transfers a file to your computer. The file can contain text, sound, art, photographs, videos, and links to other files anywhere on the Web. That's it! You don't have to know anything about computer programming languages to use the Web. The Web was designed to be easy to use *and it is!*

---

* The Jargon Page at the end of this guide explains the terms in bold.

GETTING STARTED

It's easier to get started than you might think. Your instructor will give you instructions on getting connected to the Web, and may tell you how to get a computer account at your school's computer center. An account usually includes a name or number, a password, and an **e-mail** address. Your instructor might give you his or her e-mail address as well. Write all of these (except the password, of course) on the inside cover of this guide for future reference. While you're at it, jot down the computer center's phone number—it might come in handy.

Now you will need to find out how students at your school connect to the Web. Each school has its own rules and ways to access their computer system and to get from there to the Web. Your instructor, an experienced friend, or the computer center can get you going. While you're learning how to connect to the Web, it's a good idea to take notes. The steps may seem random, and they will be difficult to remember later.

SURF'S UP!

Your instructor or computer center should have provided you with instructions on how to get on the Web. If you have these, you are ready to surf. Following your instructions, log on to your computer and connect to the web. Ready?

Before we surf the Web, let's get oriented to using the browser. The Web browser you are using looks something like a picture frame on your sceen. It will remain throughout your time on the Web. This frame contains **buttons** that allow you to do several things. In this section we'll explore how you can navigate the Web using the browser, and using what you've learned, pay a visit to the U.S. Senate's Web site.

In Figure 1 you can see what one of the most common browsers, Netscape's Navigator 2.01, looks like. If you've never seen a browser before, the buttons and labels may look a bit bewildering. For now, we'll concentrate on the most commonly used functions. Once you're familiar with these, you can take some time to learn the more complex features of your browser.

The "location" box tells you where on the Web you are (some browsers call it the "Web Page," "URL," or "Go To" box). If you want to go to another page, this is where you enter its **URL**, or address, which looks something like this:

http://www.senate.gov/
(or)
http://www.senate.gov/leader/officers.html

The first address is the Senate's home page. If you type this into the location box and press Enter, you will be connected to a Web site

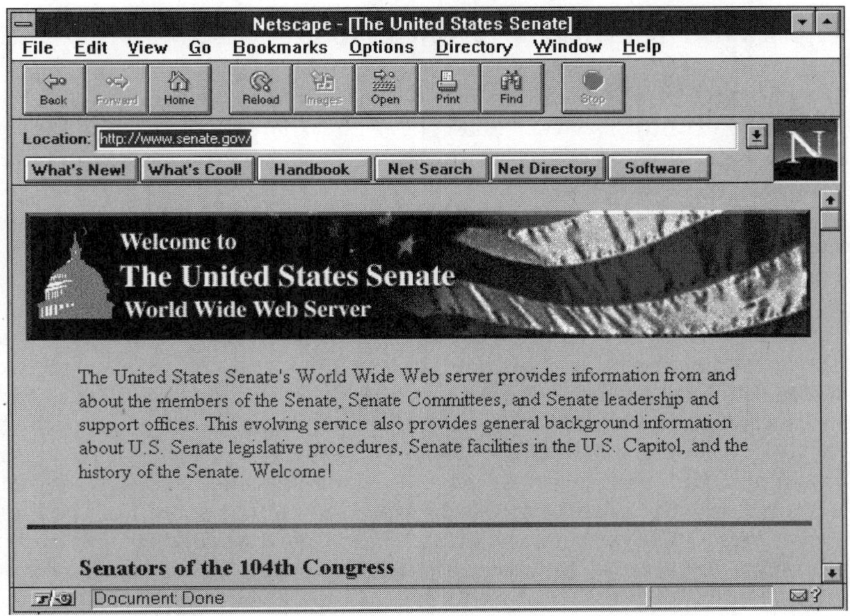

Figure 1
The Netscape Navigator Browser

managed by the U.S. Senate, where you will find a wealth of information about senators, including their official statements and activities. The second address will take you to a specific page on the Senate Web site that lists the Senate officers.

The URL usually starts with "http://" and often ends with either "html" or "htm." Sometimes it merely ends with a forward slash "/" to indicate that this is not just one file but rather a **Web site** containing many files. The "www" in the URL (newer sites may use "ww2" or forgo "www" entirely) lets you know that it is part of the World Wide Web. In the addresses above, "senate" is the name of the server, and "gov" indicates that this is a site run by a governmental agency. The area between the slashes "/leaders/" is a subdirectory on the Senate server that holds the file. The file name is "officers.html."

As you can see, URLs can be long and difficult to remember. Later, we'll describe some useful ways of saving addresses you want to visit later. Also, St. Martin's has set up a Web page that will connect you to dozens of Web sites containing information on American government and politics.

FROM HERE TO THERE AND BACK AGAIN

In the location box, type in the Senate home page URL, http://www.senate.gov/, and then hit the Enter key on the keyboard. Your browser will start to look for this site. While the browser is trying to access the Web site, you will likely see some movement in a symbol near the upper right-hand corner of the screen (in Navigator, this symbol is the letter "N" with comets shooting by). This movement lets you know that the browser is busy accessing (or "loading") the Web page you requested.

When your browser is finished loading a page, you'll see that some of the words and phrases are in color. Usually these are the **links**. Clicking on them will send you to different files at different Web sites around the world. The color of a link depends on which browser you are using and the site you are visiting.

When the Senate home page is done loading, scroll down the screen using the **scroll bar** on the right side of the screen or the Page Down key. Click your mouse on the blue text that reads "Directory of Senators (by state)." Now you should be looking a list of states and their senators. Scroll down the list and click on one of your state's senators. Click on additional links to find out more about your senator.

If you want to learn about another senator, you will want to return to the list where you started. The easiest way to do this is to click on the browser button labeled Back. Keep clicking on the Back button until you've returned to the Senate's home page. Notice that the links that you have already used are no longer blue. You can still click on them, but the color change reminds you that you've been to their pages already. Try looking at the home page of your state's other senator.

Once you've learned about your senators, click on the Back button until you get to the Senate home page. At this point, you might decide that you want to return to the page you were just visiting. The easiest way to do this is to click on the Forward button until you get there.

You may be wondering how the computer keeps track of what's "back" and what's "forward." The browser keeps a temporary list of the files you have visited on this trip. This list will disappear when you log off the computer, but it is very handy during your travels.

What if you want to go to the page you visited five pages ago? This is where the aforementioned list really comes in handy. In Navigator, click on the word Go in the **menu bar**.

File Edit View Go Bookmarks Options Directory Window Help

A list of several addresses will appear. If you click on one of them, you will return to that page. As you can see, URLs aren't easily recognizable as the addresses of their respective pages—they contain several codes and abbreviations. Unfortunately, you'll often have to guess which address is the correct one for the page you want to revisit.

Other browsers may use another system. Immediately to the right of your location box you will probably find a button with an arrow pointing down. Click on this button, and you will see a list of the Web pages you have already visited. As with the Go option, you need only click on the URL in the list you want and the computer will automatically return you to that Web page.

Sometimes you will accidentally click on a link you don't want to visit. Since Web sites that are loaded with graphics can take a fairly long time (sometimes several minutes) to access, you may want to stop the transfer of the file. To do this, just click on the Stop button. This will halt the incoming file but may leave you with nothing on your screen except the browser. After you hit the Stop button, you might want to hit the Back button to start over from the page you just left.

SAVING, PRINTING, AND BOOKMARKING

You've found the information you want. How do you move it from the computer screen to your own files? Most browsers allow you to print the Web file that you are looking at. You may have a Print button on your browser screen or Print may be listed as an option on the File menu on the menu bar. If you are using your school's computer, you may have to ask someone how to send your output to the appropriate printer. Try printing out the list of states and their senators.

You may want to save the information from a Web page in your own computer's memory or on a floppy disk. This process will vary considerably depending upon which browser you are using and whether you are on your own computer or one belonging to your school. If you are using your own computer, you can save the text from Web pages on the hard disk drive. If you are using a school computer, you may not be allowed to save files on the hard drive. For these reasons, you should always carry a disk for saving data as you surf the Web. Saving or printing these files will save time and energy when writing your research reports. Try saving the list of states and their senators.

TABLE 1

SAVING TEXT IN NETSCAPE NAVIGATOR

1. Insert a floppy disk into the computer.
2. Click on "File."
3. Click on "Save As."
4. Choose file type "Plain Text."
5. Choose drive "a:" (or wherever your disk is located).
6. Enter a file name such as "senlist."
7. Click on "OK."

You may want to save only part of a Web site's text. If you are not too experienced in the Windows environment, you should probably save the entire document (as in Table 1) and edit it later. You can copy and paste parts of the text if you are comfortable with running more than one application at a time. Use the steps in Table 2 to save selected text from a Web page.

TABLE 2

SAVING SELECTED TEXT IN NETSCAPE NAVIGATOR

1. Click and hold the left mouse button at the beginning of the text you wish to save.
2. Continue to hold down the left mouse button, and drag the cursor over the part of the text you wish to save. Release the mouse button.
3. Click on "Edit" from the menu bar.
4. Click on "Copy."
5. Minimize the Browser screen by clicking on the downward pointing arrow in the upper right-hand corner.
6. Open your word processing application.
7. Click on "Edit" from the menu bar.
8. Click on "Paste."
9. Save the file.
10. Minimize the word processing application and return to your browser.

Your browser may include a function called **bookmarks** (or "favorite places" or a "hotlist") which keeps a permanent list of Web sites you've visited and want to visit again. With this feature, you do not need to memorize the URLs of sites you want to revisit. For example, use the Back button to return to the Senate home page. Click on the word Bookmark on the menu bar; then click on Add Bookmark to save this site. The title of this page should appear in the list below the Add Bookmark and Go To Bookmark options. You may want to bookmark this page and the House of Representatives home page (http://www.house.gov/) because they are great places to find out about your members of Congress and what they are doing! Next time you go online and want to visit a bookmarked page, just click on the Bookmark menu and choose the address from the list that appears.

Bookmarks are a convenient time-saving device, but if you are using your school's computer, you may not be able to save your bookmarks on the computer's hard drive. Luckily, most browsers allow you to "export" bookmarks to a floppy disk. On subsequent visits to the Web, you can "import" your bookmarks to go directly to your favorite Web sites.

TABLE 3

EXPORTING AND IMPORTING BOOKMARKS ON NETSCAPE NAVIGATOR

Exporting Bookmarks	Importing Bookmarks
1. Save bookmarks as usual.	1. Click on "Bookmark."
2. When your session is done, click on "Bookmarks."	2. Click on "Go To Bookmarks."
3. Click on "Go To Bookmarks."	3. Click on "File."
4. Click on "File" (within the Bookmarks window).	4. Click on "Import."
5. Click on "Save As."	5. Select the desired file.
6. Enter a file name of your choosing such as "book1."	6. Click on "OK."
7. Choose drive "a:" (if that's where your disk is located).	
8. Click on "OK."	

Web searches often take longer than you expect. If a server is busy or underpowered, it may take a long time to transfer files to you. You may see a line at the bottom of your screen that says something like: "Transferring file: 50% of 20K completed." This means that the computer is working on sending the file to your computer and is half done. A file that contains a few lines of text can be sent in a couple of seconds. But a complex site, like that of House Majority Leader Dick Armey, which includes photographs and a great deal of text, takes a long time to transfer. A site like this could take anywhere from 30 seconds to several minutes depending on the speed of your computer and its modem.

WHEN THINGS GO WRONG

The Web is a very busy place, but each server has only a limited number of phone lines connected to it. If you try to access a popular Web site and all of its lines are busy, you may get a message saying that this Web site is unavailable. If this happens, you may want to try again, but don't hit the Enter button—you'll get the same message. Instead, try the Reload button. This will start over with the URL and may get you through.

Busy sites are always a concern. If you live in the Eastern time zone, you may want to do your work early in the day before the rest of the country is awake. If you live in the Pacific time zone, you may want to wait until later in the evening when everyone else is asleep. If you live in the Central and Mountain time zones, daytime hours are somewhat less busy than evening hours.

Sometimes sites aren't busy—they just disappear! This happens for a variety of reasons. Students and faculty leave schools and take their files with them, individuals change Internet connection services, or companies go out of business. The result is a **dead link**. Occasionally, you may get a message saying that the browser cannot find a particular URL. Sometimes this happens because the site is shut down for maintenance, files are being revised, or the server is temporarily out of service. Sites created by Web enthusiasts on home computers come and go like the wind. You won't immediately know if a problem is temporary or permanent. If you have a problem accessing a site, try again later or on another day. If the site is still unavailable, it's probably dead.

Your browser will have many more options than we have discussed in this section. You know enough now to begin exploring further. Experiment with the rest of the options when you have some spare time. Nearly all browsers have a Help button or command that you can refer to like a user's manual. Also, don't forget to ask the staff at the computer center for assistance.

GOING SOLO

Library research is easy if someone gives you a list of the books and articles you need. The trick is finding the right books and articles on your own. You can now get information about the Senate, but only because you were given the Senate URL. How do you find other Web sites?

There are two quick and efficient ways of finding Web sites filled with information on government and politics. The first is called a **search engine**. A search engine is a Web page on which you type in words or subjects. The engine then searches the Web for sites that contain the words or topics you're seeking. These search engines are created by private companies that often provide this service free by selling advertising space on the results pages. If you do a search on "golf," for instance, you may see an ad for a brand of golf clubs at the top of the page.

There are several very good search engines. Like any private company, they may go out of business quickly or last for years. The following search engines are recommended, but you may find others that you like as well or better.

AltaVista	http://altavista.digital.com/
Lycos	http://www.lycos.com/
Magellan	http://www.mckinley.com/
Yahoo	http://www.yahoo.com/

Try connecting to the AltaVista search engine. You will get a screen that looks something like Figure 2. Each of these search engines has many options and added features. For now, let's try a basic Web search. To perform a search, enter your key terms or topics in the box and click on the Submit button. The search engine does the rest.

Figure 2 shows the results of a search using the keyword "Senate." Note the number of Web pages found using this search: about 100,000! Indeed, the most common problem with search engines is finding *too much* information. Some search engines allow you to narrow these searches by using conditional statements like "Senate and United States." Some rank the resulting sites according to their "fit" with the terms you entered. Others operate using preset categories.

You can also find Web sites that allow you to use several search engines from a single location. Two that are currently popular are:

1. Search Com — http://www.search.com/

2. Savvy Search — http://www.cs.colostate.edu/~dreiling/smartform.html

It may take some practice and experimentation to master efficient search engine techniques, but it is well worth the time invested.

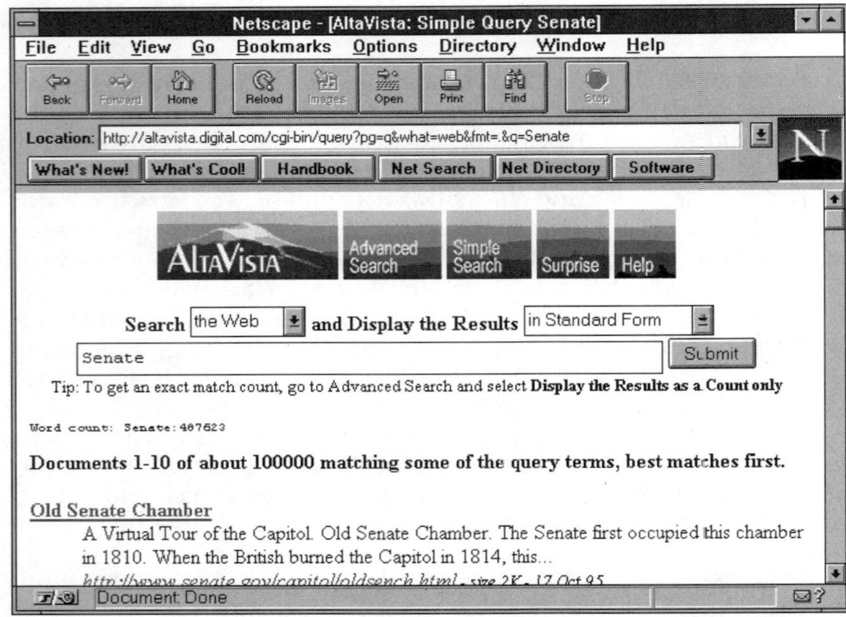

Figure 2
An AltaVista Search on the Term "Senate"

Some strategic planning will make your use of search engines more productive. Before you even begin to use a search engine, you may want to brainstorm on the major terms associated with your topic. If your topic is the writing of the U.S. Constitution, you might write a list of the names, places, books, concepts, and government institutions involved. Then you can perform a systematic search by using logical operators such as "and" and "or."

Spelling is very important when performing a search. If you type in "Cogress," the search engine will look all over trying to find "Cogress." You and I can recognize common typographical errors, but search engines cannot.

When you are looking for a narrow topic, be as specific as possible. Try more general terms if more narrow searches come up with disappointing results. Don't give up easily. Persistence will often pay off great dividends.

The best alternative to a search engine is a reliable and quality **links page**. Essentially, a links page has already done the searching for you. There are many links pages that exist solely to point you toward sources of political science information. These are often created by the political science departments of colleges and universities, political parties, activist groups, research organizations, and government agencies. Unsurprisingly, some are better than others. When you find quality links pages, bookmark them for future reference.

St. Martin's Press has established the St. Martin's Political Science Links Page that you and anyone else can use to find the most reliable and authoritative sources on the Web. You can use these links for all of your current and future classwork. You can find the St. Martin's Press Political Science Links at:

http://smpcollege.com/smp_govt/ps_links.html

Bookmark this location as soon as you arrive at this site. It will be very helpful later on.

The links you follow may lead you to a site that is not part of the Web. It may be an FTP (File Transfer Protocol) or Gopher site. An FTP site is a location for copying someone else's files. Someone may have a copy of the Constitution in his or her computer's memory but may not want to put the entire document on a Web page. Instead, an FTP site can be set up so that visitors can copy the file more efficiently.

The Gopher system is a predecessor of the Web. It links sites together but lacks most of the appealing graphics and complex options available on the Web. FTP and Gopher sites can be made to look very similar to a Web site, and the better Web browsers allow you to visit these sites. You may not even notice you are at a Gopher site unless you look at the URL.

Researching Politics on the Web

The Web and the greater Internet serves many purposes with regard to politics. It is a great medium for dispersing information on academic research, governmental and political organizations, statistics, and historical documents. It also provides a forum for debate and the expression of opinions. These are all very valuable roles. But if keeping these roles separate is challenging enough when using traditional library resources, it is much more difficult on the Web.

With just a little learning and effort, anyone can set up a Web site. Everyone from the president and Congress to radical hate groups use the Web to transmit their ideas on politics. Keep in mind that while some sites contain balanced and factual information on politics, other sites may be terribly biased or present misinformation as fact. Even respected sites like the White House or those established by members of Congress may put a self-serving spin on their information. Just because a Web site (or **newsgroup**) is sophisticated or impressive doesn't mean the content is reliable.

Keep in mind some criteria when deciding whether to follow a link. Government and educational institutions are usually, but not always, more reliable than commercial sources and not-for-profit groups that *may* be political advocates. You can tell the difference by their URL.

TABLE 4

Recognizing URL Sources

http://somebody.edu	an educational institution
http://somebody.gov	a governmental agency or unit
http://somebody.com	a commercial service
http://somebody.org	a not-for-profit organization
http://somebody.mil	a military organization
http://somebody.net	an Internet service facility

Just because a source is a political advocate or has a certain bias does not make that source useless. It is important to know what various groups think to understand the contours of American politics. Use such sites as sources of opinions but not necessarily as sources of factual information.

The political and governmental resources available on the Web are tremendous. It is essential to have a strategy for finding what you want in as little time as possible. The St. Martin's Political Science Links Page is a good starting point. You should also try to find other links pages put out by colleges, universities, and their political science departments.

Several sites sponsored by news organizations and libraries provide searchable databases. Like search engines, they allow you to use key words to do your research, but rather than searching the Web, the engine searches through the organization's archives of articles, photographs, and recordings. These can provide a direct route to material that would take hours to find in most libraries.

You may want to save or print Web pages while exploring Web sites for later use in writing essay assignments. Be sure to follow the same rules regarding quotations and citations that you would with any other source. Write down the name of the author, title of the document, the date, and the URL of the site as you find information that you need. Sometimes the author will not be listed, in which case this information may then be excused. This is the Web equivalent of an academic citation, and your instructor will want to know where you got your information. Your instructor may be able to direct you to a resource for citing sources online.

ST. MARTIN'S POLITICAL SCIENCE SUPPLEMENTS ON THE WEB

Before we start this leg of the trip, let's turn to the map in Figure 3. St. Martin's Press has created several Web pages as a supplement to our political science textbooks: the home pages for St. Martin's Press, our American Government textbooks, and the American Government supplements on the World Wide Web. There is a home page for each text, its table of contents, and several pages based on the book's preface. From each table of contents page you can link your browser to other files that have the Web research exercises. These assignments will in turn link you to St. Martin's Political Science Links Page. This page is like a compass that can point you in many directions from which you may leave St. Martin's Press and go to dozens of places on the Web with the information necessary to complete the assignments.

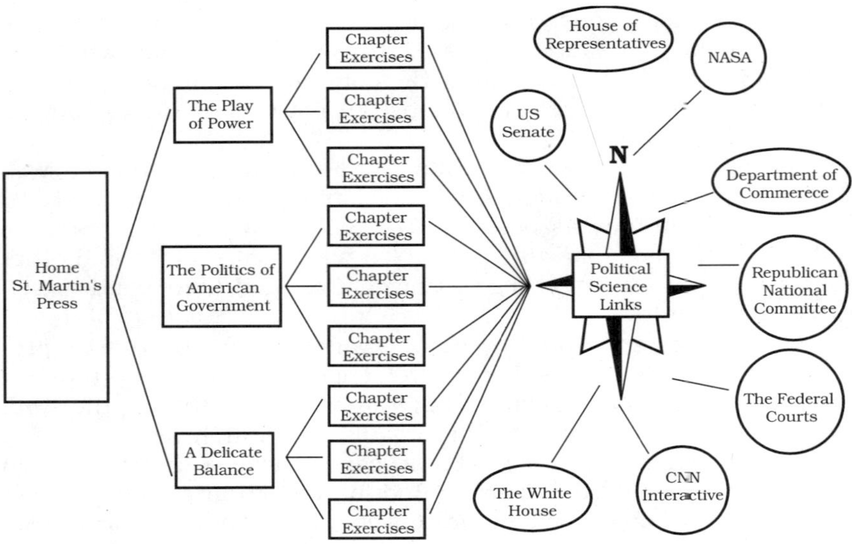

Figure 3

Each chapter listed in the table of contents of your text is linked to a set of Web exercises on a separate Web page. Your instructor may assign one or more of the several Web research exercises for each chapter. You will read the assignment, find the necessary information on the Web, and submit a report to your instructor.

To begin the exercises, start at the home page for your textbook and link through the table of contents to the appropriate chapter's exercise page. You may want to bookmark the table of contents so that you can return to it directly on subsequent visits. Write down the exercise or print it out, so that as you surf the Web you know exactly what you are looking for. Now you are ready for the research to begin.

The exercise page will link directly to the place on St. Martin's Political Science Links Page most appropriate for that research exercise. From here, you may go to some of the best Web sites concerning politics. Don't assume that you've reached the only place you need to visit just because the links page sent you there. Some exercises ask you for specific information that can be sufficiently researched at one site. Other exercises will ask you to go in directions that interest you. Almost every site has additional links to other sites. Explore these links, and strike out on your own. When you find additional sources of information, bookmark them so you can return later.

The links page is not meant to be comprehensive. It is intentionally selective and represents the most authoritative and durable sites. For this reason it represents only a small fraction of the many political sites on the Web. Use a search engine, other links pages, and the recommendations of friends to find more sites.

An example may make the mechanics of the exercises a little clearer. Your instructor will assign one or more of the research exercises for each chapter either in the syllabus or in class. One of the exercises reads as follows:

> Visit the Web site of one of the following activist political groups. Who are they? With which problems or issues are they concerned? Why do they engage in "unconventional political behavior" rather than mainstream political activities? What tactics do they use to achieve their goals?
>
> Act Up
> Anti-Defamation League
> Earth First!
> Greenpeace
> Operation Rescue
> WHAM (Women's Health Action and Mobilization)

To make a choice, click on the name of a group. This will send you to the Organized Interests section of the St. Martin's Press Political Science Links page. From there you can go to the Web site of this group to find the necessary information and answer the questions posed in the exercise.

When you are done with your Web research, it is time to write your report. Your instructor may want this in print or sent via e-mail. The report should look essentially the same in either format. If you use e-mail often, you know that typos and grammatical errors in casual communication are widely committed and tolerated. However, an e-mail report should be as clean and coherent as a printed report.

Once you have made it this far, you will have the knowledge and skills needed to discover the wealth of information available on the Web. There is much more to learn about browsers, Web sites and political research. This guide is only intended to get you started. If you want to find more you can consult one of the following texts:

Campbell, Dave and Mary Campbell. 1995. *The Student's Guide to Doing Research on the Internet.* Reading, Massachusetts: Addison-Wesley Publishing Company.

Gagnon, Eric, ed. 1996. *What's on the Web?* Fairfax, Virginia: Internet Press.

Hahn, Harley, ed. 1996. *The Internet Yellow Pages,* 3rd ed. Berkeley: McGraw-Hill.

Jamsa, Kris and Ken Cope. 1995. *World Wide Web Directory*. Jamsa Press.

New Riders Publishing. 1996. *WWW Yellow Pages.* Indianapolis, Indiana.

Pfaffenberger, Bryan. 1996. *Web Search Strategies.* New York: MIS Press.

THE JARGON PAGE

Bookmark A file that marks a Web page for a direct return on later visits.

Browser A software package that allows the computer to present the Web to the viewer as text and graphics.

Buttons Pictures and graphics that direct the browser to another location and may resemble push buttons.

Dead links Web links that connect to a site that no longer exists.

E-mail Electronic mail. Notes that can be sent from one computer system to another.

Home page A Web page that serves as the entry point for a Web site.

HTML Hyper-Text Markup Language, the computer language used to create Web sites.

Link A word, phrase, or graphic that, when clicked-on, automatically sends you to another place on the Web.

Links page A Web page that contains links to other Web pages.

Menu bar The horizontal list of options found near the top of most Windows applications.

Modem The computer's device that allows communication with other computer systems; the computer equivalent of a phone.

Newbie Someone who is new to the Web.

Newsgroups Electronic forums for discussing particular topics.

Scroll bar The vertical bar on the right side of a windows screen that allows the user to see documents and images larger than the visual area of the monitor.

Search engine A Web site that allows visitors to search for other Web sites related to particular topics.

Server A computer dedicated as a source of Web, FTP, Gopher or network files for transferring to other computers.

Surfer, surfing Someone who is experienced at exploring the Web. (Exploring the Web)

URL Uniform Resource Locators; the address of Web sites.

Web site A group of interconnected computer (HTML) files located on one computer.